Finding
Forgiveness

**kevin
mayhew**

To Dick and Margaret Hyett,
gratefully remembering your support
and kindness

First published in 2005 by

KEVIN MAYHEW LTD
Buxhall, Stowmarket, Suffolk, IP14 3BW
E-mail: info@kevinmayhewltd.com

9 8 7 6 5 4 3 2 1 0

ISBN 1 84417 365 8
Catalogue No. 1500769

Designed by Chris Coe

Printed and bound in China

Contents

Introduction

Smug, self-righteous, sanctimonious – that's how some people view Christians, but in my experience they could hardly be more wrong. No doubt there are Christians like that, but most I've come across are quite the opposite, all too aware of their failings. Indeed, if there is a danger, it's of brooding too much on one's faults and weaknesses, dwelling on them to the point of morbid preoccupation. It's impossible to stand in the presence of God, focusing on the love, grace and goodness revealed in Christ, and not to feel acutely conscious of all that is wrong in one's life – and it's important that we feel this sometimes, in order that we might attempt to put things right. We should not, however, struggle through life with a feeling of unworthiness, still less carry with us a burden of guilt or shame. Nor should we feel that changing for the better is down to our own efforts alone. At the heart of the gospel is the assurance that God accepts us as we are, with all our imperfections. His love is not conditional on our goodness, dependent on our keeping faith – it goes on reaching out day after day despite meeting rejection and disobedience. Yes, he wants to see change, and he will be at work in our life every moment striving to make that happen, but he will not condemn us if and when we fail. Ours is a God slow to anger, swift to show mercy, steadfast in his devotion towards us.

The prayers in this collection attempt to articulate some of those ideas, expressing the frustration we may feel at our recurrent weakness but also giving voice to the assurance of God's patient and unfailing forgiveness. Some are general, some more specific, covering such themes as wealth, pride, environmental responsibility and social action. Why are they couched in the form of poetry? The answer is very simple. For me, verse – and rhyming verse in particular – is able to express things in a way that prose alone cannot quite match. The rhythm carries the reader along, the rhyme gives a sense of completeness and final resolution, and the two in tandem make the words easy to remember and repeat.

These prayers, then, or poems – call them what you will – offer words through which to acknowledge our faults but they offer also a reminder of God's awesome and amazing grace. They are intended, quite simply, to help you pray.

Nick Fawcett

Lord, Forgive Me

**Father, I have sinned against heaven
and before you.**
Luke 15:18

Lord, forgive me, I am weak,
seldom do the things I seek,
rarely serve you as I should –
wrong prevails instead of good.
By your grace come make me whole –
mind and body, heart and soul.
Where I'm false help me be true;
wash me clean and make me new.

Taking Stock

**Fashion a new and unblemished heart within me,
O God; imbue me with a true and faithful spirit.**
Psalm 51:10

Where are the vows of long ago,
the promises I made,
the faith and trust I used to show,
the vision I displayed?
Where is the eagerness I knew
to follow day by day;
though all else failed to still stay true
and serve you come what may?
Where is the life I swore to lead,
the love I aimed to share,
the gentle word and thoughtful deed
that showed how much I care?
Lord, for all my lofty dreams
I've fallen so far short –
to walk the way of Christ, it seems,
is harder than I thought.
Make up in me the strength I lack
to stay true to your call,
for I would offer something back
to you who gave your all.

Pride Goes Before a Fall

In humility, count others better than yourselves.
Philippians 2:3b

For the foolishness of pride
and the hurt to which it leads;
for the value I've denied
to my neighbours' words and deeds;
for the failings I condemn,
and the flaws I'm swift to see,
all those faults I find with them
yet can never spot in me;
for dismissing every view
running counter to my own,
overlooking people's gifts,
having time for mine alone,
grant your pardon, God, I pray;
call me back, before I fall;
help me take the Saviour's way
and respect the worth of all.

True Riches

Do not amass earthly treasures for yourselves ... instead accrue treasures in heaven.
Matthew 6:19a, 20a

In a world awash with greed,
occupied with serving self,
where the overriding creed
honours gain and worships wealth;
where we rarely seem content,
always seeking one thing more,
so much time and effort spent
adding to our worldly store,
gracious Lord, help me to see
where true riches really lie:
show me that your love is free,
something money cannot buy.
Teach me, then, each day to toil
not for treasures of this earth,
but for that which will not spoil:
gifts of everlasting worth.

Celebrating God's Goodness

**I have come that you might have life,
and have it abundantly.**
John 10:10b

Have I failed to live as I ought to,
to serve you as I should?
Have I flouted your will and denied you,
and turned my back on good?
Am I thoughtless, selfish and greedy,
concerned with self alone,
expecting the hungry and needy
to get by on their own?

The answer, Lord, hardly needs saying –
all this is true and more:
my life far too often displaying
mistakes I've made before.
But though such betrayals may grieve you,
they cause you hurt far less
than how often I undervalue
the ways you long to bless.
You offer me life overflowing,
more blessed than words can say.
Lord, help me to thank you by showing
how much it means, each day.

Faith in Action

**I tell you the truth, whenever you offered
service to the least of individuals,
you offered it also to me.**
Matthew 25:40

I'm not an angel, nowhere near,
I often go astray,
but though my faults are all too clear
I try, Lord, to obey.
Avoid what's evil, strive for good,
that's been my daily aim –
to live the sort of life I should
in keeping with your name.
But now I see that this alone
can never fully do;
instead it's how much love I've shown
that matters most to you.

If, when I saw a friend in need,
a person in despair,
I paid their plight sufficient heed,
enough to show I care.
My times of worship, hymns and prayers,
each have their part to play,
but only if my life declares
the truth of what I say;
if what I am and what I do
stays faithful to your call,
in showing love not just to you
but equally to all.

Flawed Discipleship

**I do not understand why I act as I do.
For I end up doing the things I hate
rather than the things I want to do.**
Romans 7:15

I've failed to love you, Father,
as much as you love me,
content to offer, rather,
a feeble travesty,
a going through the motions,
a playing of the part;
too often my devotions
not springing from the heart.
I truly mean to follow,
but other voices call;

discipleship proves hollow
as yet again I fall.
Commitment proves expensive,
temptations lead astray,
demands prove too extensive,
self-interest wins the day.
Lord, hear my supplications,
have mercy and forgive;
see past the limitations
that scar the love I give.
Remould, renew, refashion,
that I might learn your way,
responding with the passion
you show to me each day.

Learning to Love

If I speak in the tongues of ordinary people
or of angels, but do not have love,
I am nothing more than a blaring trumpet
or a clashing cymbal.
1 Corinthians 13:1

I try so hard to love, Lord,
to reach out in your name;
to know the worst in people
but cherish them the same.
I strive to show compassion,
to show I really care –
yet measured by your goodness
such love cannot compare.

For what I give is partial,
a prize that must be earned;
its constancy dependent
on whether it's returned.
The love you give, in contrast,
is free and unreserved;
poured out with no restrictions,
although it's undeserved.
Lord, come and work within me,
transform my heart of stone,
until the love I offer
grows closer to your own.

Love Divine

**We see love most completely in this:
not in us having loved God but in he
loving us so much that he sent his Son
to put right our relationship with him.
God is love; all those who live in love
live also in God, and he in them.**

1 John 4:10, 16b

I have no claim on your love at all,
    no grounds to seek clemency;
I mean to serve, but repeatedly fall,
    my faithlessness plain to see.
The vows I've made, commitment professed,
    all seem to have been in vain,
as faults and flaws so often confessed
    return to haunt me again.

You see the worst, all my ugliness,
all that poisons deep inside,
but still you love, always eager to bless,
refusing to be denied.
No words, O Lord, can begin to say
how much I will always owe;
no sacrifice even start to repay
the mercy and grace you show.
I give you thanks, bring my all to you,
amazed that such love can be –
so rich and full, so constant and true,
so priceless and yet so free.

Stewardship of Creation

The heavens proclaim the glory of God:
the universe testifies to his handiwork.
Each day witnesses eloquently and each night
communicates knowledge, without need of speech,
language or any other voice.
Psalm 19:1-3

You've given a world, Lord, of untold delight,
    that moves me to worship and praise;
that speaks of your glory by day and by night –
    so much there to thrill and amaze.
The peak of a mountain, the shade of a tree,
    the colour and scent of a flower,
the peace of a river or wrath of the sea –
    each gives me a glimpse of your power.

The laughter of children, the crunching of leaves,
or delicate song of a bird,
the hum of a city, the whispering breeze –
in so much your voice can be heard.
Forgive me, I pray, the indictment I share
for failing to steward this Earth,
neglecting to give it due honour or care,
and losing a sense of its worth.
I squander resources, betraying your trust,
yet somehow I don't seem to learn.
Lord, help me to treasure this world as I must –
that others might share it in turn.

Good Intentions

**It almost seems to be a law that whenever
I intend to do good, evil is there as well,
for while inwardly I delight in God's law,
I see a different law in my body battling with
the law of my mind, enslaving me to the law
of sin that dwells in my members.**
Romans 7:21-23

Lord of my life, have mercy I pray,
I've failed you again, abandoned your way.
My vows I've betrayed, commitment denied,
intending to serve, I've strayed from your side.
Deal kindly I ask, redeem and renew,
see not what I've done, but all I would do.

God's Way and Ours

Just as the heavens are beyond the earth,
so are my ways beyond your ways,
and my thoughts outside your thoughts.
Isaiah 55:9

For turning faith to outer show,
to what I say and do,
my focus more on what I know
than truly knowing you;
for thinking you can be contained
by my poor reach of mind,
assuming truth can be explained
or rigidly defined;
for all the ways my faith is flawed
and understanding skewed,
I ask your pardon, gracious Lord,
and beg to be renewed.

Amazing Grace

Christ demonstrated his love for us like this: through offering his life for us even though our lives were steeped in wrongdoing.
Romans 5:8

Lord, I come to worship, not because I should,
not to claim I'm worthy, virtuous or good,
not because I'm special, different to the crowd,
having any merit, reason to be proud.
Rather, I come humbly, conscious of my need,
knowing I've been faithless, false in word and deed.
Day by day I stumble, miss the goals I seek;
though I mean to serve you, inwardly I'm weak.
Lord, I can't deceive you, hide what's deep inside,
yet you bid me welcome, arms extended wide.
Gratefully I worship, coming not in fear,
but responding gladly, thankful to be here.
I will try to follow, walk the Christian way,
not because I have to, but because I may.

Giving Our All

**The Father will honour all those
who serve me.**
John 12:26b

Take the life I proffer,
loving God, today;
all the gifts I offer
all I think and say.
What I am and what I do,
these I give you now.
Lord, I want to serve you –
show me where and how.

Renewed Commitment

**For the sake of your name,
lead and guide me.**
Psalm 31:3b

Lord of life, direct my ways,
help me love you all my days.
Though my faith is flawed and frail,
though I all too often fail,
take my heart, my hands, my feet –
reach out now to all I meet.
Teach me how to serve and when.
Guide my footsteps, Lord. Amen.

The Vital Ingredient

**You shall love the Lord your God with all
your heart, all your soul, and all your mind.
This is the first and greatest commandment.**
Matthew 22:37-38

I offered songs of worship,
knelt down to you in prayer.
I sought your will and guidance,
and read your word with care.
I went to church each Sunday
and pledged to walk your way,
resolved to serve you better,
determined to obey.
To everyone around me,
I must have looked the part –
yet one thing, Lord, was lacking:
true worship from the heart.

Glimpsing God's Presence

Be still, and know that I am God.
Psalm 46:10

Lord, today your voice is calling,
lifting thoughts to things above;
life is wonderful, enthralling,
touched by your unfailing love.
Suddenly I see the beauty
often hidden from my gaze,
so I come not out of duty,
but with glad and grateful praise.

Lord, I sometimes fail to value
all your blessings as I should;
slow to make due time to thank you,
blind to so much that is good.
Days are lived in such a hurry
there's no time to stop and stare;
joy is crushed by weight of worry,
happiness obscured by care.

Lord, today I come rejoicing,
vowed to waste your gifts no more;
bringing praise and gladly voicing
what I should have voiced before.
Pouring out my adulation,
scarcely knowing where to start,
with a song of exultation,
Lord, I thank you from the heart.

A Faith That Shows

**Let your light shine before others,
so that they may see the good deeds you do
and give glory to your Father in heaven.**
Matthew 5:16

O Lord, I want to praise you,
your holy name confess,
your mighty deeds acknowledge,
your awesome love express.
I want to give you honour,
to lift your name on high,
yet somehow words are lacking
however hard I try.

I want so much to thank you
through all I say and do,
to so live out the gospel
that all may know it's true.
I yearn to give you glory,
to help your kingdom grow,
yet though I strive to serve you
it rarely seems to show.

I bring you, Lord, my service,
deficient though it be;
aware my faults are many,
I come still, joyfully.
For though I'm weak and foolish
and know you but in part,
you look beneath the surface
and see what's in the heart.